BONE SEEKER

Bone Seeker

Chris Haven

NYQ Books™

The New York Quarterly Foundation, Inc.
Beacon, New York

NYQ Books™ is an imprint of The New York Quarterly Foundation, Inc.

The New York Quarterly Foundation, Inc.
P. O. Box 470
Beacon, NY 12508

www.nyq.org

First Edition

Set in New Baskerville

Layout and Design by Raymond P. Hammond

Cover Painting: Edward Munch, "Towards the Forest (The First Human Beings)," 1896, watercolour, crayon, black on parchment, 302 mm x 500 mm, Munch Museum, Oslo, used under a Creative Commons Attribution 4.0 International Public License and written permission of the Munch Museum.

Library of Congress Control Number: 2020945287

ISBN: 978-1-63045-068-7

Bone Seeker

Contents

Bone Seeker

bone seeker
radioactive substance that tends to accumulate
in the bones when it is introduced into the body

—Dictionary of Energy

The Boy Shows the Girl His Country

Over here are trees that burst into flower.
You are always beautiful here.
This is something you have too but spell differently.
Those are as stinky as you've imagined.
Lovely the way you say that. Sounds remade.
We eat these tubes of meat but usually they taste better.
Our night isn't dark. Do you have night over there?
You don't have to be afraid of the color of this sky.
Sometimes there are fireworks but it doesn't pay to wait.
You've never had fruit like this.
Most of the bees have gone away.
We're afraid of what people think. We laugh at everything.
Go ahead. Make any gesture you want. Not that one.
An honest man registers with the government.
This is the year we count things.
Don't take our electricity too seriously. Just keep back.
Best look in every direction when you cross.
We don't dance that way or comb that or put our lips there.
That would probably get plucked but it's no big deal.
It's true sometimes they return with no legs.
Some people gather those and put them in their windows.
Yes they are beautiful and sometimes we shoot them.
You must hiss at that creature for it to depart.
The tiny things will kill you.
They can't be stopped, so don't worry.
We dig holes for those and insert them when we're done.
We're so glad you were here. Speak of us in your accent.
Carry the news of us far. Make us new.

How Nuclear Fusion Works

I was in love with you for thirty-eight seconds last night.
Your hair all dressy and the way your smile fuzzed your eyes,
My gestures so big we're lucky I didn't smack you.
I spoke in hieroglyphs, you answered cuneiform.
Then pop, time for my love to leave. You're not the only one.
There's a girl I love for twelve seconds, the pink of her
Laptop, her fake-red hair, at this distance, a dream.
There are seven houses I love. They're smaller than you think.
I love their outsides only, the lives their walls imply,
Windows framed by shutters black, useless and lovely.
Little yellow house, if I lived in you my love you could not contain.
I love old women and men too, how their lives intersect
With my memory of how once I believed the world waited.
I have loved the color green and uniformity. Because my love is fickle
I have loved raggedness, admired the deception of the weed.
Chairs—the right ones—I love like nobody's business.
Sometimes I love the asshole coach, in that long wait for the hot
Moment of attention. Salesman, I have loved your big handshake,
The strength it wants to deliver my hand. Never mind the pain
Of returning blood. The list is long: sound of the woodpecker,
Golf-cart girls, checkerboard patterns, even the cheapest
Stained glass and every freckle. But the time, so limited.
I bestow my love widely and often, almost always secretly.
It's not made for the light of day, this sniper field of laser
Beams, housed in a cement-walled building, all aimed at a single
Point. It conjures a star, brighter than several suns, then dies
In a trillionth of a second. Someday, all the world will be powered
By these tiny stars. For now, it has to get by however it can.

Bounty

After the event, much food is left.
Take the food, we tell the people.
The people are young and we want to give
the young everything. There is so much food
they can't all eat it or stuff it into their pockets.
One woman lingers. She is a large woman.
She may be poor. I have been poor.
We look at the food in the same way.
It is wrong to waste this food. We must find
containers. Take all you want I say,
but only what you won't spill.
It's good advice she says,
hypnotized by the bounty.
This is a blessing. It should be saved.
Soon the caterers will come
in their jackets and take it all away.
Time is short.
I go in search of containers.
When I return, the young ones are gone
except for the woman. She kneels
wiping a paper towel on the floor.
I spilled it, she tells me.
That was the one rule you had, I say.
I know, she answers. I can tell
she misses the spilled food more
than she will enjoy the food she kept safe.
It is good she is cleaning up.
I leave much food behind.
When I walk out of the building, it is spring.
In my neighborhood, the magnolias
have already begun to wilt.
They are too much. The ground can scarcely hold
the sad ears of their petals.
There are never enough baskets.

Ocean

Is it time to be ocean,
or is it time to be shape.

Measure by volume
by weight by mass
by salt content
by the fishes in you by the fishes in you that have died
by weed by the rising water.

We'll lose our cars our homes our dignity
all the pictures we haven't printed.
The ocean wants to see its pictures
bury itself in sand wants to know what it's like
to get a sunburn feel the skin peel know heat.

The only performance you are capable of giving
is the one unawares.
Do something shameful.

The sand is losing, they say,
the sun is losing, there's only so much more time
and then everything will be different.

You will be your own ocean.
You are already your own ocean.
You are the one eating everything.
You are the one being ruined.
You are the one doing the ruining.

When the water rises it's good for the water.

What's on the ocean's list.
Bread milk whales ships pirates treasure.
Didn't we just get some the other day?
How are we always so low on treasure.

The ocean wants one of those jackets
with its name stitched on the pocket
and a plastic ID to hang around its neck
maybe a little sheriff's badge and a stick horse
moon dust and a poster for the rec room.

The ocean's mother has died.
Put flowers on her grave.
Put her in the ground standing up,
to make room for the dead yet to come.

Take a picture
but don't develop it don't print it
don't post it don't ever look at it again.
Someday, we will all have been immortal.

Preserved even before we've died,
remembered before we're forgotten,
before these shorts we're wearing have gone
out of style, before they find a fabric
that doesn't pull your hair out.

Someday we might have hair again,
all sorts of sexy hair again, we have so many things
let's want the things we do have.

Unless it's love, or a bicycle, or ice cream,
or a bicycle made of ice cream, with a banana for a seat.
All the ocean wants is to have a seat.

Even the ocean doesn't know why all the storms.
The ocean doesn't know any words for the color blue.
The ocean didn't want to wreck your ship.
The ocean has never been baptized.
Doesn't know what sleepless means.
Misses its mother like a folksong.

We are at a feast which doesn't love us

after Tomas Tranströmer

Nobody will clip her nails. They are made of the same things as her bones. Strong stuff. Not like the rest of her. You need the tool shaped like the jaws of a snapping turtle and both of your hands. Press harder. This is not hard enough.

It musn't be sad. Not when the room is red and the Bibles are stacked on the end table. Every pill she needs is there for her, even some she won't. You'll never know the difference. They chisel letters and numbers into them and sometimes make you cut them in half. The colors only mean that they couldn't think of anything else to do for you.

Today the plate holds half of a sandwich. Sometimes it's eggs. You'll make whatever's left in the kitchen. Yesterday it might have been pizza topped with black olives. Tomorrow you won't know what you will have left. The plates are empty. Sometime later, the plate will come back full.

Palmyra

The Lion of Al-lāt has fallen.
Eyes of stone have fallen,
nose, blocks of teeth,
tongue of stone,
mane of stone,
the gazelle between his paws.

Gone the strange gods
the old hands
assembled, carved,
created in mere image
mere earth.

~

The new men don't worship
the old stones.
Most gods want the other gods destroyed,
or the evidence of the gods,
or the worship of them,
or the evidence of the worship.

~

The old ones in charge of the stones wouldn't tell the new ones
where they were. The old ones did not believe in the gods but
they believed in art. The dead are dead but the art of the dead is
dying. Destroying art is destroying dead men. All men have been
destroyed, or waiting to be destroyed. Even the youngest art, espe-
cially the youngest. It's tiring work all this killing, all these different
kinds of dead.

~

The children gather at the new school in the old place.
The teachers show them a lion and they think only lion.
They show them gazelle and they think only lion.

~

Old ones worship the chisel, the young the hammer.

~

lion of al-lāt

           reassembled
in a new city
              fully
        fixed
arranged for
          new children
   dissembled wars

  any true god
        wills
      its own toppling

The City of Aleppo

The city of Aleppo fell, and so did my mother.
She dragged herself across the floor with her one
good leg, the other newly useless but still,
I imagine, she considered it a good and useful friend.

You may have seen the children of Aleppo
if you own a computer. Their faces were streaked
with blood during the fall, which made them more
like children, though they will never be child again.

My mother was not so much like Aleppo
except that after her fall, she was also streaked
with blood, and she was also trying to reach
her phone, to call to strangers for help.

The city of Aleppo has a long history, stacked
with ancient tongues and tablets and gods and horses.
My mother also had a history of calling for help.
It took her eleven hours to get to the phone.

The people of Aleppo had access to Twitter,
a social media platform designed to connect
people from all across the world because surely
connection is good, is an end unto itself.

Of course they say that pride goeth before a fall,
but the fall comes anyway. So many mothers,
grandfathers, so many useless legs in so many
cities and countries across a newly connected world.

A child of Aleppo sits on a bench in a city square,
a city built on top of the ruins of itself.
We can't know how long the child will sit.
Some things are measured not in time, but stamina.

I can't tell you how Aleppo will end but the end
of my mother's story is a broken-down door
and a trio of policemen she loved until the day
she met her true end, because there's always another end.

Now is the time when the poets call for optimism,
where the people of Aleppo are reminded that even
a short life is filled with beauty, no matter the end.
Remind them that archaeology gets it wrong.

Sometimes the bones you see can remind you
of the person you want to be. Sometimes you
are the one being called. Sometimes we're not
alone. Sometimes the horses stay buried.

Wednesday Night Lightning

Wednesday night lightning hit
the three tallest buildings in Chicago
but this isn't Wednesday

~

Tonight they're looking for the bombers
they're trying to figure out who is master
by the way the bodies lay on the floor

Something unspeakable about the way the bodies
are configured, which one wore the vest,
how our lives change if a woman triggered the bomb

On the news we learn how to make bombs
on our screens our thumb and fingers scroll
the lies and the truth, and no way to tell them apart

~

Three buildings are enough for a skyline
A skyline is enough to fall in love
Love is enough to fall

~

The lightning strikes, and leaves us
with our buildings

We want our buildings to outlast us
we want our work to outlast us

We want the grandfather to make the plans
the father to continue the work

The son to hold the chisel, keep chipping
long after we've all stopped believing
in the plans

23

~

Wednesday is a day in the week
that has never known Friday

Night is a darkness that we once believed day separated

That's us up there in the picture, we all think,
our lives lightning, electricity, a photo opportunity

~

Sometimes we are cloud to ground
Sometimes we live without a sound
Sometimes we are electric

~

Tuesday forgot what Friday did
too busy piling stones
on top of the roses

The dark hangs heavily

I have taken to calling the darkness sweet.
It is the way I keep it out. It is
the swish of broomstraw across the floor. It
is a lonely sound only if you forget how sweet.
Just a little taste will tell you how it is.
But must you? Child, you don't want to taste it.
You don't want to let it inside you, to
open your mouth to the darkness, let it sleep
on your tongue. It will lie there, in
a ball where it can't be caught, tricked by the
lie of how sweet it is, by the coolness
of the space around it, the coolness of
its own hate. Hate wants to sleep, sound and snug,
curled in the dark of your unawareness.

Golden Shovel, from the fourth stanza of Gwendolyn Brooks' poem "Truth":
Sweet is it, sweet is it/ To sleep in the coolness/ Of snug unawareness. The title is
the penultimate line of "Truth."

Bead Board

A man with a red truck came to fix the sagging
bead board ceiling of my front porch. The roofers
sent this man because of the terrible job they did.
This man, they said, was a man who would fix it all.

The man had to duck to get in the doorway.
His tired eyes looked up, acknowledged the sag.
The man said he'd had throat cancer. He raised an arm.
Skin puckered where lymph nodes used to be.

His eyebrows had filled back in fine as a baby's.
This man said he was shaken. He didn't know
what to do about the sag. He picked up a drill
and said he'd put some bolts in. Will it work I asked.

He looked hurt. Maybe not he said. I told him go ahead.
He raised his puckered arm and drilled four ugly,
shiny, silver bolts into the nice old bead board.

I knew he was going to die. That's the way these things go.
I also knew that those bolts would never hold.
Nine years later, the boards do sag. The way they work,
it appears, is they overlap, one with the other.

If one goes, you have to take them all out. Start over.

Bone Seeker

Marie Curie sometimes slept with a jar of radium by her pillow.

First time she sees her bones
ring curved black on her finger
uncracked stone
this her truest wedding day

~

find the smallest thing
collect as many as you can
put it in your body & he
will put it in his & tell him
you see it & he will tell you
he sees it too. Do this
for the rest of your life.

~

I will place you near what needs to be killed
I will have you
1600 years

~

half of a life
half of a couple
half of a theory
half of an element
half of a prize
half of a miscarriage
half of a daughter
half of a parent
half of a lover
half of polonium
half of radium
half of a grave

~

call it a laboratory
take notes on everything
every light every drop of water
everything that moves.

~

Lit isolation
Lit seeker
Lit touch
Lit bonejar
Lit skinblue

~

A lifetime later
measure them
touch wand
to paper

click
click
click

Lovers Resolve, Charles and Emma Darwin

Charley says to Emma I will write you
a treatise

           Emma says to Charley I will say
           a prayer for you

one that explains how
it's only natural

           that you might see
           your way to truth

selection and how
these traits of mine

           one that shows how like
           a god

will help us
ascend

           in this complex
           life

into a state of perfect
adaptation

           we can be oppositely
           wound

here on this living
earth

           even on the other side
           of death

O my darling
isn't it time we

           come together,

      advanced—

Flannery at Lourdes

They took you to Lourdes where the water
was freely given. You refused and then
assented. You prayed but not for your bones
and entered the grotto carried by two,
one able body on your left and one
on your right their hands holding you steady
in the *piscines,* and dipped you naked
into the water. The waters were cool,
your body held still for sixty seconds.
All around brewed the sick and ambitious.
You thought of contagions, your humor able.
The only prayer that escaped: for your book.
You prayed for the words and to be given
only that which should be freely given.
Isn't this how we all should come, naked,
attended by one at each side, carried,
borne, lifted into the water, infirm,
surrounded by the unwell, asking God
only to be given the right language?
Put it in the water. See if it walks.

Janis Joplin's Eulogy to the Graduating Class of Thomas Jefferson High in Port Arthur, Texas, 1960

You're not all dead yet but soon will be.
Truth is, it's hard for me to muster
all the hate I used to have.
I used to think you made me
lonely and I could hurt you
with all the love in my life.
I burned. I wanted to smoke you.
Longer dead than alive now,
that's where you'll all be, man—
Might as well wear feathers.
I was trying to figure
where the fault lied,
but my secret: I wanted it all.
No reason for you to have
all the good stuff.
Did you live good lives?
Did you do good work plumber,
bus driver, refinery worker?
Have lotsa babies, get the right
husband? Ever find the good
drugs? Lotta different kinds . . .
I'd take them again if I could.
See, here you get to see
possibilities. I coulda died
seventeen times before that hotel room.
If that one didn't get me I had fifty-
six more waiting. I see them like stars,
constellations of all my deaths.
You'll get to see yours soon enough.
The hardest thing for me here?
I don't get to sing.
You? You won't get to do
whatever shit you liked to do.

Elegies on the Passing of Celebrity

Darken the house lights—time for the montage.
The stars watch the stars, and us, we look on
from our world separate, ageless, a kind of admiring.

Here's a dead cowboy. His hat a ghost town, a tumble
of brush, a haunted player-piano, scrolling
those holes, tinkling jubilation to the wind.

This one, born the same year as my mother.
They play your songs and I use your voice,
the one with swagger, before the rattle of pills.

And you, my father thought you beautiful.
I listen for magic. You speak frozen flowers.
Why does a man tell his wife another is pretty?

They say you hailed from Nebraska, but those curtains—
all California. The jokes and smirks, the way the men
pinched their slacks. You made sunny all those dark-home nights.

You, my mother said, weren't pretty. You should have stayed
small-town. Those kind of men and their business cards
must be refused. You were a lesson to be learned.

Now the dancer: the boy, the man that never was.
It's your shrieks we love, the way your body cuts
the air, the way your feet light what here can't be lit.

All of you, so easy to love, so easy to tarnish.
Drink and drugs, sex and guns, fiery crashes,
and one spectacular leap from a building.

Popping light bulbs. White-hot moments. All the flickers.
Let us all celebrate—every high and low light. Clap for us,
in some dark, velvet theatre. And when we exit,
let us all exit with a little shatter and dazzle.

Interrogative[1]

The phone[2] rang[3].
"[4]Is that[5]
the little[6] lamb[7]
I[8] made?"

1
This is a short poem.
Short poems evoke
more than appears.

2
A phone is
a device for communication.
It used to ring.

3
The phone's ring in the past
might be described
as a bleat.

4
Quotation marks
indicate a speaker.
Readers like this.

5
This has
an unclear
pronoun referent[a,c].

6
Little is an important
word. Nobody wants
a lamb large.

7
William Blake wrote
the poem "The Lamb."
He might've been serious.

a
Pronoun referent
is now confused[b] with
pronoun reference.

b
Sometimes a new confusion
becomes the way
we do things.

c
Unclear pronoun referents are
wrong in composition.
Poets love them in poems[d].

d
A poem is not meant
to be understood.
A poem is a lamb.

Some writers prefer
the absence[8]
of quotation marks.

Only one of these[?]
can be
the poem.

Not all of these[?]
has to be
the poem.

If all of these[?]
are the poem
then ignore the notes.

One footnote
must always be
left blank.

———————————————

8
Everybody thinks
they know which god
they believe in.

Five Ways of Looking at a Mushroom Cloud

in response to Rebecca Campbell, I Am Hideously Complex 4

I

The white and orange hot heat
of the explosion, melted filmstrips,
faces and flappy projectors,
the five times you vomited at school,
the one face that teacher and student,
frozen every time, made.

II

The blue of it
the sky of it
the yes of it
the too bad of it
the gay of it
the pilot of it
the why not of it

III

It's the little punching bag in the back
of everyone's mouth.

It's a tiny little boxer
in an Old Testament minor prophet cave.

It's a speed bag, bippity bippity bip,
reverse, negative exposure.

It's a mouthpiece boiled in water and sweat.
We're all training for something.

IV

Once the Ancient Grecian ruins weren't ruined and they weren't
actually white but polka-dotted, and there was one that was not
multi-columnar but uni-columnar and they made it of
smoke and split pebbles and they wore robes around it and en-
gaged it in dialogue about its nature and teased it and chortled
with knowing looks and their laughs laughed the smoke away and
all the pebbles fell straightaway and buried those sons of bitches.

V

A few steps from a wooded trail, buried
in a crackle of leaves, a fungus top
orange as an encyclopedia frog,
a wonder uncaring and unbidden,
never ridden a train or been to France,
stanched bleeding or looked into a canyon
or stuck seed in the crevice of a tooth,
or published a scholarly article,
uploaded a video demonstration,
or cried for the want of a color
it never knew existed outside itself,
for a small dirt-borne tragedy, buried,
memorialized, with no witnesses.

VI

the dark of it

The Difficulty of Simultaneity

When lightning struck
that little lake
next to the gas station
in the mountain pass,
it was the last chance
for services.
Our tongues tingled
for miles.

The Defenders of the Birds of Our Region

The birds of our region like
        the crunch of strange bugs.

The birds of our region complain when things don't change
and then again when things stay the same.

Nobody likes their art. They paint study after study of water towers.

        The birds of our region have an uncomplicated theology.

They do not, and this can't be stressed enough, appreciate windows.

The birds of our region do not know how to describe their grief.
They expect you to remember everything about their wings.

They will hold you accountable for your own despair. They refuse
to address the lifespan of meaningless conversions.

They will not quiet their children. They have all given up
their landlines. They embrace irony. All their nests are derivative.

The birds of our region have forgotten how to dance,
only remember their nostalgia for the dance.

The birds of our region accept payment for reviews on Yelp.
They freelance. They review the books of their friends.

They congregate in gymnasiums. They have burned all the pews.

They will not stop selling their dreams. They know
which car is yours, and they take dead aim.

The birds of our region are tiresome about their candidates.
They mistake their freedom for the freedom of others.

The birds of our region believe there is a season for everything.
They believe they have done nothing

        that needs defending.

What Water Does in Pennsylvania

There is a flood watch in Pennsylvania. I have not driven the state before and I wonder, who put all these mountains here? How am I supposed to know what water does in Pennsylvania. This suitcase I have packed is so heavy I can't lift it into the trunk. The case is filled with suits, a clown suit, a kangaroo suit, a president suit, a suppressed voter suit, a jockey's colors, a suicide suit, an active measures suit, a gamer's suit, the suit of our last dying dream, and socks. It is unliftable because I have forgotten something, or will soon, or have left behind the feeling of belonging, among other things that won't fit into the suitcase. The rest stops in Pennsylvania are nice though, except for this one I've chosen, which has only the bad kind of fries and the weapons-grade hand driers are all broken. It's a wonder it took so long to put wheels on suitcases, books in backpacks, but I still don't understand the tunnels through these mountains, or the significance of Valley Forge, or why America's suitcase has found its way into my hands, this thing I carry but cannot, lift, that keeps asking me for advice and never following, my country a barge that must be lugged into a mountain, a mountain made of suits that probably never fit anybody in the first place.

Who among you is afraid to go into the dark and empty spaces?

(asked by a reporter of Iraqi street children after the U.S. offensive in Iraq, 2003)

Who among you is afraid
   to go into the dark
          and empty spaces?
My boy, three, awakens eyes
shut with rage
        voice
a slice of glass
     he is on his knees
nothing would calm him
        but now
my hands lay him down
     they take him to the dark
               places
a hand to his back
     and one hard
at his side.
        Follow the man
  with the big hands
through the bombed buildings
          spilling wires
a cough
   of dust.
  A smear
of ash.
           Take me
to the places that used to be.
  Rusty threads.
     Black water pipes.
  You must walk
carefully
     I am told of unexploded
bombs.
    There are bullets
       that sprout wings
          and fly

to the heart of you.
　　　　Bring no light
to the dark
　　　　there is no such thing as good fire.
You will know people
　　　　you will never know a friend.
I am your guide
　I will find your hand
　　　　　　　by the heat it stirs.
　　　　I have gone
before but never
　　　　was it this bad.
　The tracks
　in the dust
　　faint
　　as rumor.
　　　　Who among us is not
afraid to lead a child
　　　　to the empty spaces?

Say This in the Coming Storm

When the sky threatens to split
apart tell the child it's never killed
when the ground begins to shake
tell her it's growing season
when the shingles peel off in the wind
tell her they are becoming birds
when lightning cracks say it's the best way
to see when the foundation trembles
recount the comfort of Pentecost
when the water rises say all
creatures are held safe when she sees you
trying to hide pieces of the sky
tell her it's scripture when your mind turns
to a child's when you look at her
and you can't remember anymore
what to say, ask her to stay with you
just until morning so you might show
her the sky is still wedded to the earth
even the sky knows the important thing
is to stay together through the storm.

The President Declares Disaster

Sometimes he wonders if he signed
Up for this, presiding over rising
Disappointment, winds, ruin.
Sometimes his sleeves are rolled,
Other times he stares down tornadoes,
Squiggle in his brow.

One day he wants to say no.
Why always yes.
Why is it always so much.
Why does steel have to twist that way.
Tree, do not bend. Sinkhole, why sink.
Tsunami, why tsu. Malaise. Hunger—

It's all yes. It's all quake. Your stomach,
My son, is a disaster. Your life, your car,
Your lovely wife. Disasters.
Your children, your love, your flab,
Your droop. Disasters. Your leanings,
Your desires, your interpretations of scripture.

Disasters. That beard. Simpleton's haircut.
Please, he says, bring the paper so I can
Sign. Disaster. The way you treat
Your mother, the music you listen to,
Love you make. The sad chemistry
Of your breath. The dollops. The stain.

Radar blips. Comma, unblinking,
Spins toward us all.
                    He takes to his plane,
Fistful of souvenir pens. Refuel in the air.
Steady now.
        There's no place to land.

Tornadoes in the Distance

We sit and wait for them to
drop.

Our legs are in the dirt,
crossed.

But they may be uncrossed,
too.

The Songbird's Song

I worry about the songbird. She disappears, one note at a time.

The songbird sings a complicated song. Devotion and clear glass and water. Dips and trills and sharps. It delivers unmistakable pain. Each night, of this I'm certain, the songbird's song is one note less.

I don't know how long the song has been. It's hard to measure what's being lost.

Maybe a hunter waits, cuts down one trailing note at a time. I can't see the bird, or hunter. I smell gunpowder. Each night a bullet.

If I asked you to hear the songbird's song, I'm not sure you would hear it. I'm not sure I would hear you.

I hear the song and open the window. The cold, the stirring leaves. I listen for the lost notes and worry that in the strain I miss the notes that have not yet gone. One thing is taken away at a time. This may be happening everywhere.

On this night, I hear a single note. I close the window against the silence and wait. Nothing left to do but sing.

Jonestown

I kept wondering if it was an accident
if they didn't know
            what the
        purple
            held

I kept
        wondering if the parents didn't know
what the children
            were drinking

I kept wondering
    why their tongues didn't stop
            the poison

I
  kept wondering
    why the guy in the glasses
made up a god
            that hated children

I kept wondering
            about the rows
    the neatly stacked
shirts and jeans
            limbs and hair
sometimes children
                beneath

45

I kept
        wondering
    how long they lay
            awake how long
        until they
                trickled away
I
    kept
wondering
    who the mixers
who the servers
            who the stirrers

I   kept   wondering
    about   the   path
how   many   steps   how
    long   the   lines   how
many   children   how   many
    thought   they   were   waiting
for   something   good   at   the   end

Ikeptwonderinghowthebodies
            arrangedthemselvesdid
        thechildrenliedown
firsttobecoveredor
        didtheyslip
orwheretheypulled
                    under

46

I if kept you wondering only if drank you half would the still cup die

I k e p t w o n d e r i n g w h a t t h e d u s t w o u l d h o l d

       I kept
            wondering if God
 was watching
I kept wondering
    was it accident
        it was wondering
           what was I
                I was it
                      I kept it

The Word We're Looking for is Sorry

It's a child's board game. It's the hardest word. It's apologetics. It's
mea culpa. It's responsibility. It can be a bullet. Fonzie can't say it.
It can leave a mark. Hearts ache for the lack of it. You can't eat it. A
man shouldn't say it. It starts with so. It cannot kill but it can bury.
Even with vast eyeglasses it cannot see. It dreams. Maybe it rhymes
with starry. Brenda Lee's version is a fake. Chicago has trouble with
it. So does Elton. It might be buried. It can give. It cannot receive.
It cannot patch a pair of jeans. It's embarrassed to be written in
a card. If it's withheld it can build a nation. The love of it kills
soldiers. There's so much it wants to do. It never gets to do every-
thing it wants. It lives not on the tongue but in desire. It is subject
to whim. It lacks vigor. It cannot build consensus. It doesn't know
what else to say. Perhaps it has gone missing. Let's give up. Let's do
something else. Let's go build a mighty nation.

Sandman

In the country without
snow the children
roll balls of sand
for the body.
They find casings
on the ground
for buttons,
shrapnel for arms.
For eyes they can use
eyes, if they want.
And when on top they place
the beret, don't think
for a minute
this creature does
not grin and
come to life.

The Iceberg and the Volcano

Today the little girl fell into the volcano.
She was looking for her mother.
Her mother had been frozen in an iceberg.
The iceberg had been sinking ships.
The ships had been taken over by pirates.
The pirates had been trying to feed their bloated children.
The bloated children had to eat piles of cash.
The piles of cash were sad. They were worth less today.
The somewhat poorer men stole from the even poorer.
The even poorer stole little girls and put them on ships.
When the little girls get hurt, the poor men are happy.
One little girl got away.
The volcanoes heat the earth's crust from the core.
The icebergs are melting.
Soon, all the mothers will be free.

The Woman Tells Her Life Story

The woman kept her life story
in a plastic ice cube tray in a drawer.

Each cube held a different jewel.
The story could only be told by her.

There was nothing of value.
Every jewel in it was semi-precious.

She had only sons. They didn't care
about the life story kept hidden away.

This turned out to be fine with her.
The collection in the tray wasn't for them.

What pleased her was the way
she'd thought to arrange the jewels.

Middle Space

I.

Nothing in the room.

II.

Nothing in the room but *glass* and *sky*.

III.

A *plant* has been placed in the room.
It thinks it is a *tree*. Its leaves are *waxy*.

IV.

The fibers of the carpet in the room tug on shoes.
They want *nothing* to leave.

V.

Someone has *watered* the plastic tree.
There is a *puddle* on the floor of the room.

VI.

A *plaque* appears, naming the tree.
The name of the tree appears to be spelled wrong.
The water has left a *stain*.

VII.

Pink *petals* have appeared on the tree.
It is unclear how they have been attached.
The tree *appears* to have been lengthened by one handswidth.

VIII.

Room.   Sky.   Glass.   Tree.

IX.

A person in the room *laughs,* does not look at the tree.
A petal disattaches, settles on the person's *head.*

X.

Petals and leaves attach and disattach
in an order that *intercedes* glass and sky.

XI.

There is a thin blue light of knowledge at the *core* of the tree.
When the tree is gone, the room will be empty of the tree.

XII.

The tree is *gone.*

XIII.

The plaque remains, and the stain.

I Am the Watchman

The streets are quiet.
I sit on a lawnchair
on your roof.
You have a nice house.
I am self-trained. Unfit.
Your roof creaks.
From here, I can see trouble.
That bush of yours
needs trimming.
That daughter of yours
is headed for bad choices.
I can take care of that.
This is a good view.
I can make the shot.
Hear that cricket?
Crickets mean trouble.
I am thirsty but I will not
leave my post.
I am here because
you want me to be here.
You have a nice car
but not as nice as theirs.
There is a boy.
He is nearing your house.
I can make out the figure
by the starlight.
I have no idea
who he is or where
he might be going.
Leave him alone?
This is the time
you've been waiting for.
He's looked in your window.
I can get down
off this roof.
Say the word.

He is walking away.
Here. I'll unlock your door.
The wind noses in,
rustles the fringe on your rug.
I hear footsteps.
He might be circling back.
What shall I do?
All your doors are open.

The Best Among Us

I didn't know I was a policeman I thought I was just walking along I saw you and I recognized you but I had to take out my pad I didn't know I was a policeman and write you a ticket for what I don't know and you went away mad. I didn't know I was a policeman but I was compelled to bring order I picked up some trash and I think I registered a bicycle I didn't know I was a policeman. I reported to headquarters I didn't know I was a policeman and they answered me back in numbers and so I looked for what I needed to respond to. I've got this uniform and a gun probably loaded I didn't know I was a policeman and people walking around and I couldn't tell which of them were guilty and then all of them started looking guilty but I didn't have bullets for all of them so I turned and I didn't know I was a policeman shot a tree. This seemed to confuse people I didn't know I was a policeman kicked that same tree to make it look more guilty and that seemed to work but my feet hurt so I put down my gun and took off my uniform and wasn't sure where the uniform stopped and so I took everything off and just ran away. If you see me running watch out there is something behind this that's bigger than you or me don't get in my way or try to stop me I am a policeman.

Phony London

I went to London and all the sights were fake they were large and
colorful but fake every one of them every person an imposter the
cars fakes the horns fake buses fake and the squirrels the tiny squir-
rels and the fake river with the fake swans and the fake theaters
where Shakespeare never went and the taxis going in their fake
directions the tube wasn't even underground I could see the seams
everything jangled and the knowing looks I caught the bagpipe
guy on a smoke break and that abbey was a nice try but fake all the
same and the protesters with their fake causes and empty tents the
books empty no juice in the batteries for our cameras to take the
fake pictures of the fake scenery get out of town with those sheep
and the phony phones the play money the postcard queen don't
even get started with the museums and the blatant fabrications
every plaque reminds you of what you're not really seeing on the
entirety of time's falsified continuum my bones got exchanged
for fake ones the whole time walking fake to the marrow and on
the plane coming back which was probably a fake too they were
replaced again those bones with my own but some had been rough-
ened and some had been shined by God knows who such that it's
hard to shake the notion I might have come back an entirely fake
and completely differently feeling person.

The Fence

Today the fence went up around a building I should have known. The people I'm in charge of asked me why and I said I knew and it calmed them. I'm supposed to know what happened because I wear the same clothes as the people who decide. Don't be afraid of the fence and the earth behind it is supposed to move. There will be corridors and walls to come. I say these things and they happen in their heads. They come back the next day and they say I lied the fence is growing. I said I know but it's still okay because there are paths. I go from the building I'm in and the fence follows me to the next building. I think I better go home and the fence takes to the highway. I feel like it's my fault if I go home but I do anyway. My wife is asleep. She's been asleep for eight days. The fence is around our house now. There are still ways around. You can still walk around. I can see the paths from the window. It will still be okay. We will all be okay. I am here, saving us all.

Instant Replay

after Anne Waldman

Back back before the days days of instant replay replay things only happened happened once. If there was an explosion explosion the concussion of it concussion of it had its moment moment in time time and then went away like smoke smoke in the air. Those in the area would turn turn their heads heads and that was their one chance to see see what they had already felt felt. Before the camera camera nobody knew just what a horse's legs legs looked like in motion motion. Only an artist could imagine imagine the un- un-imaginable. Now the video video camera is our artist artist stuck in a loop loop of the same thing thing so we believe believe everything happens again again. This time each new time it's different it is. Pause and zoom zoom. Freeze freeze the moments. Call them real real. We know so much more more than we did before. We are so much more real real. When someone blows up, it's time to cry cry. Cry.

Poem for the Recent Tragedy

How could _____ have happened here?
What kind of a _____ could _____ such a thing.
The _____ was heard miles away. People have lost their _____.
_____ are still being totaled.
Everything will be _____. _____ is still _____ in heaven.
The _____ will not win. The church bells will _____
Observe a moment of _____.
This kind of _____ has never been seen before.
We have seen the face of _____.
The _____ will not be ruled by the _____.
The _____ will not win.
_____ shall not prevail.
Nothing can break the _____ of America.
We will get to the _____ of this.
The _____ will not _____ justice.
_____ will be a new day in America.
The sun will _____, people will _____ to their _____.
We will not be _____.

Word Bank (Words may be repeated):

Bend   Best Supporting Actress   Bigots   Blank   Cash

Cheat   Coca-cola   Conviction   Cured   Deserving

Explosion   Faithful   Flag   Hip Hop   Honeybees

Lite   Maker   Melons   Milkshake

The National Football League   Played   Reverence

Spin   Swagger   Sway   Underserved   Undeserving

The War Photographer

The War Photographer expected more
glamour out of life. His wife hitched
her beauty to his danger, an eighty dollar
Leica camera and a studio in the heart
of the jungle. It didn't take long.

When War was a baby they posed him
on a bearskin rug. He was so scrumptious
it made you want to poke your eyes out.
In grade school freckles riddled his face.
Underneath spread the dynastic grin.

Every time War left the studio—
whirl, and the stink of glory, and fire.
The War Photographer's wife lettered
the orders for eight by tens, five by sevens,
and the wallet sizes that would be scattered

from the sky like leaflets. Or ashes of leaflets.
In middle school War grew into his features,
mustard hair, foxhole dimple in the chin.
The War Photographer took extra time
brushing away the acne pocks and red-eye.

Now, the senior pictures are over.
All the trendy new locales have been sealed,
delivered. His class has graduated, backdrop
to the disaster of the War Photographer's life.
Nobody wants to look at the pictures anymore.

The War Photographer unscrews the bulbs,
sweeps the canisters and shells to the corner.
His wife has cancer now in her hips. She walks
like a clumsy sidekick. At first he was happy—
it gave her something to hate besides him.

Now the War Photographer knows his wife
loves her cancer more than she loves him.
They rarely talk about what went wrong with War,
or love, or the close-ups of suffering,
or any of the other things that will never return.

The Outlaw Pose

In any picture of brothers
you can tell the dapper one,
hat the angle of Saturn's rings.
Each necktie inexpertly tied,
one so fat it doesn't matter.
The older is the better killer.
Thin fingers, each a born trigger.
Your lips would know the names
of these brothers if you lived then.
Part of you would have feared,
all of you would have loved
the milkyness of their eyes.
The whiskey in the picture
more than mere prop, or
maybe everything's just a prop,
wanted poster for all our doors.
It's the younger one you relate to.
Top lip strains an overbite.
You recognize the way inadequacy sits
next to his more vicious brother
like you tolerate your most private stink.
The younger's hat's a better fit for a mule,
but he plods along. The hapless
ones he kills end up just as dead.
The boys' shoulders slope,
neither large enough to carry a long life.
The ears of the older one tilt—
he will hear the one that gets them,
but the little brother, he will never know.
He will die in a hush. He's been leaking
gunpowder from his ass since the day he was born,
each day down a lucky accident,
biding the spark that will take out him,
his brother, the horses they rode in on.
But for now, it's time to look at the camera,
light splashing across stupid foreheads,
wide as a country, blank as law.

Discussion Questions on the Dead Man, Sophomore Literature

1. What is the main idea of the dead man?
2. Identify and discuss the Christian influences of the dead man.
3. Discuss the code of loyalty in the dead man.
4. What qualities did the people feel a good dead man should possess?
5. How is the dead man certain that he is dead?
6. Discuss the battle between good and evil in the dead man.
7. What is the central conflict of the dead man?
8. Discuss the role of fortune in the dead man's life. Cite examples.
9. Is the dead man a hero? Why or why not?
10. If the dead man could tell a tale, what tale would he tell?
11. Discuss the role of reputation in the dead man.
12. Discuss the behavior of the dead man in each of his battles.
13. What attitudes and actions led to the dead man's downfall?
14. Is the dead man the most important dead man?
15. Write an obituary for the dead man from the point of view of the dead man
16. What is the dead man's favorite part of being dead?
17. If the dead man were a flavor of ice cream, what flavor would he be?
18. Compare and contrast the dead man with your father.
19. What is the best lie you've ever told a dead man?
20. Be the dead man. What's it like?
Defend your answers with examples. Be concise.

Tombstone

Once I had a tombstone.
I put my father's name on it.
The tombstone survived.
I put the tombstone in the grass.
The grass turned to dirt
   then back again to grass.
I put my mother's name on it.
My mother survived.
I put my brother's name on it.
My brother survived.
I put a lyric from a song on it.
The song survived.
I put my name on it.
I have survived.
Around the tombstone
   many graves grew.
I have brushed dirt away.
I have talked to the tombstone.
It has not answered back.
I am not sure the power
   of a tombstone.
Perhaps I have mistaken
   the order.

The Second Pig

I had to build a building.
I dug stones from the ground
with my bare hands.
They didn't seem big enough.
They were all I had.
I didn't have a ruler.
Concrete would have helped.
I spat in the dirt,
Sealed up the cracks with mud.
When I ran out of pebbles
I took sticks. When I ran out
of sticks I thought why not
and used leaves. I built
the building around myself.
I put some grass on the top
and stepped back to have a look.
This was decision time.
It looked shoddy and poor.
I looked at the sky.
Something's coming, I thought.
A blue like friendship,
a wisp of white horizon.
I wish this was a better
building, I said into the air.
I sat down on the dirt floor,
inside these sad sticks.
I am just a pig, I said.
This is the best I can do.

Uses for the Appendix

Conversation piece

Paperweight

Meeting place after the bomb

Tea cozy

Weakside help

Erotic dream cache

Emergency tie tack

Hamster wheel

Sudden joy recalibrator

Bowling trophy

Saferoom

Shuttlecock

Hut for a backup god

Noah's ark for bacteria

Hairnet

Sin box

Bait

Spare key holder

Psychometric standard

Some of the above

Fake heart

Lie factory

Bookmark

Casket for the person you think you are

Same as everything else

Scarmaker

The Black Hole Uploads a Match.com Profile

Tall, dark, and massive. Introverted. Could stand
to lose some weight. Been burned by relationships
in the past. Bent, but not broken. I am a survivor.
Afraid of getting too close. Very observant.
Nothing escapes me. Not into parties. Prefer a quiet
atmosphere. Some say I seem inscrutable.
I do have feelings. Never let them show. Tired
of keeping it all in. I just want someone like me.
Who gets me. It's been a very long time.
But I suppose it's all relative. Be my event.
Let me be your future. Your singularity.
Show me what can't be seen. Show me
that I exist. That I matter. Light me.
Unbend me. Let me show you
my mouth. My horizon.
Come. Let's get lost
in each other.

The Cake Girl

Everybody loves the girl who builds cakes,
The red of her hair, the way her fingers move—
Empires and Eiffels and volcano mounds,
Scaffolding and wire and lights to be eaten,
Golf balls, footballs and the head of Raymond Burr,
Wheelchairs, a Slinky and Fogerty's gravel,
Everest, Hillary's step, a full-sized Sherpa,
Basketball, pyramids, Mike Lupica.
Name a shape, she can bake it in a cake:
Handgun, a file, Leavenworth and Peltier.
These are cakes and they must be eaten.
She builds them with her oven and magic.
Magic happens when reality meets flour,
Heat meets egg, batter meets our girl's tongue.
Sugar never as sweet as our girl's song.
Cadillac, Slot Machines, Grizzly Adams,
Whale sized whales, baby seals, the Exxon Valdez,
Stacks and stacks of single-breasted cancer cakes,
Maps and terrains and rivers to the belly.
All roads lead to the belly, nothing beyond.
She wears glasses, our myopic cake girl.
She'll roll a big cigar cake—all her cakes
Must be bigger than big, so she can see them—
Bigger than our imaginations,
Bigger than our nations and presidents,
Bigger than our smallest security.
You believe your tongue can feel fingertip
Traces, accidents of skin and humanity.
This day's full of nothing and celebration.
You are being called to cakes, enormous cakes.
Eat. Two-fist them. Get bigger. Swell. Get born.
It's not too much to ask to candle every day.

Carry On

I roll my socks into the case. I roll my pants. There is a place for
everything. I have seven desires and I roll them separately, tucking
them into corners where I can. I am going on a trip. There will be
trees and strange music. I leave room in the case to bring things
back. There is one thing I put in the case that nobody knows about.
It is the thing that will make me change. I have never removed it,
but it's there. It's not made of fabric so it's hard to roll. When I re-
turn I will have left something behind. I will tell you of the people
sleeping on the sidewalk, the woman who forced a sign on me.
Hungry it said, and I knew what she wanted. She knew that every-
one brings the thing to her city, the thing they never take out of
their case. When I'm away from you I'm never sure where I am.

I left something behind. A sign, strange music.
Nobody knows about the city, separately sleeping.
Everyone brings room. Everyone is removed, not made of you.

A Thousand Sexy Wives

after Ander Monson

They walk all over town, carrying movies in their hands, skin like wine and cherries. Their feet stipple the sidewalks and roads. The husbands are lost, or they are by their side, or they are lost. They walk. On cobblestone streets, historic stone roads grouted with grass and weed. They walk up hills, ankles wobbling. They cannot be slowed. They are lonely and committed to their sadness. They are sexy as old wars, hearts empty as a movie set, empty as a diamond, empty as geography. These banded women, their drowsy, wanton honor. They are relic and untouchable. They move older than direction, under timelapse skies. Their bodies urge them to the tallgrass field with a thousand junked VCRs and microwaves and plastic refrigerators convalescing where the frogs of this world hide, parting the blades of grass, waiting to sing to them.

Winter Tomato: To Depression

I love you like I love the winter tomato.
Hothouse panes and magnified sun.
I love the medicated tomato and you,
the strings and the meal and the thin,
pink heart leached of color, and I love
not knowing where that color went.

I love how you communicate in bubbles,
inscribed in a child's drawing, cramped
lettering inside, toothpick projects stubborn
and haphazard, ignoring the wide page
anyone else could use. I love depression
and white space, gifts sprawling and refused.

I love how you love me with the percent
of brain that Einstein used. Magnificent,
but kept in check, a chalky theory
and a board that demands erasure.
I love the end of the week, janitors,
the wet cloth that washes away.

All of this I cut into neat slices
on my sandwich because it's all I need.
No more struggle remembering childhood
tomatoes, a red that pops from foreheads—
those are long past, I know, and this world
is better. No one cares where the color went.

We Could Use Some Milk

I try to convince my wife the guy on tv is Death.
He's so pale and that hat. Must be Death.
Too obvious, she says.
I give up because we have no milk.

I drive the road that's potholed because
they don't fix roads of poor people.
I go to the store where the rats are.
I'm waiting for a Forerunner to back out.

I want that exact space.
It backs up like backing up is a disease
that must be suffered slowly.
Nobody has ever backed up in the history of life.

This guy is the first. He's showing us all the way
and it's like murder. Finally this guy's life mission
is over and a girl with blond curls rides her shopping cart
down the ramp. This is what everyone should do.

I love this girl, even though she might go home
and cyberbully some other little girl
to jump off a water tower like she's
the 4A State Champion of It's All About Me.

Before I get in the store there's a fake pumpkin
patch with green carpet and real pumpkins I suppose.
I remember it's fall and I'm so happy.
I don't buy a pumpkin.

I find everything on my list plus some treats.
I'm ready to be impatient with the line
and the checkout girl but she's pretty good.
We share a fondness for Oreos.

In the parking lot some genius has shoved a tiny
cart into the back of a large cart. It's too much work
to fix, I decide, so I put mine sideways
and don't pay attention to wherever it drifts.

When I get home I accuse my wife
of not telling me it's the first day of fall.
She said it's not, that it started at three o'clock.
I say that doesn't even make sense, and she agrees.

Purple Berries

One day a child showed up in my house.
He came up to my chin, not a baby at all.
I wondered what I had done to cause this.

This boy told me he was hungry
so I poured him some sugared cereal.
I think I used to have a wife and maybe

a dog because there's a little house out back.
There's plenty of room here I tell the boy
and as he slurps the cereal he looks familiar.

I remember the joys of sloppy eating
so I poured a bowl and made a lot of noise
with the milk. I've always wanted a father

I say to him and he says I think you got that
mixed up a little and I said what'd I say.
He said I think you wanted to be a father

and I said yes, maybe there is a difference.
Let's be fathers I said, putting my arm around him.
We'll go make things and then we'll leave them.

That's the way I got here he said. We spent
the night in a tent by a foamy river.
All that water in the river knows where to go

the boy said as if the water was separate.
That sounds good to me I said but I meant
the way the river made it hard to hear.

We ate some berries and he told me which ones
he thought were poison but it sounded like a guess.
I ate the others anyway and so did he.

These taste like nobody's ever eaten them
he said, and we had some good, purple laughs.
I would be proud to be your father I said.

He asked me why, was I good at ruining things.
I thought back to my previous decisions
and said yes, son, it's really my best thing.

Stupid Baby Cardinal

Stupid baby cardinal hangs on to the bush.
It will learn to fly I tell my boy—it will.
The red bird in the tree won't look me in the eye.
Embarrassed of his son. Even the bush knows
how to be beautiful three weeks a year.

Stupid baby cardinal sings one note. Its father flits
about, brushing the sound from the air.
You are made of wing. Come to the tree.
Leave the bush behind. Swish swish swish.
Trust me I tell my son. This bird will learn to fly.

All birds learn to fly. There's never been one bird
in the history of this confused world that didn't.
Maybe this is the one, my boy says.
Maybe this bird is the one you've been looking for.
The one you can, with your presence, keep from flying.

The moon in the sky of the day.
Blue has forgotten how to be blue.
Stupid baby cardinal sings a single note.
We never see it all. Note. Sky. Moon.
It speaks to no one. We all think it speaks to us.

Stupid baby cardinal has not moved.
Ugliest bird I've ever seen.
I want to help it. I want to educate it.
It won't even shake the branch.
It thinks the world was made for him.

I give the bird an ultimatum.
Be gone. Let the dark take you but be gone.
You don't even know what's coming for you.
The beak opens—Wolves perk.
The bird thinks he's learning to sing.

Morning—No trace. No nest.
No father above. A fat squirrel pokes around
the tree because of what he believes tree to give.
The night has always known how to fly.
I want to cut the bush down. I want to save it.

My boy is made of husk, night,
cardinal, and what can be taken from him.
I am made of stupid and moon.
Sometimes the moon opens like a beak.
Sometimes the moon stops singing.

Pocket Walnuts

after Dickey

Clickingly he walked as a child
Down the winding farm road,
Lined with a God-blank vision.
He dug a scattering of holes
In the ground he pronounced tree.

Those trees ticked up through their eyelet
In the sky and flecked the ground
With sweet black walnuts. Pail-sprinkled,
Cream and sugar, ice and salt he cranked.
His arms grown strong and muscle-pure.

When he finally went to town he took
A deck of cards and a country grin,
Broken-toothed and a tongue set
Firm, indented on the roof of his mouth,
Meat uncured and hard to harvest.

Then it was time to forget trees,
Wrestle the broken-downest car
That ever drove a county lane.
Patch kit in the trunk. He learned to fix,
Tricks he tried to use later on me.

Now the trees are too old to give
And the sky is dark with fathers.
I have a crease in my mouth same as his.
He puts a hand on my shoulder,
Tells me he's tired of my elegies.

He never told me about his trees
That didn't last, only the strong ones
He shook from his pocket. I wonder
How I can tell this father from another.
If I'll know the touch of the gambler's hand.

At the celebration dinner,
We wait for something holy to be said.
The years place another ring on the logs,
Wrinkled casts. We trust there's a hush
Inside. Split them and they shine.

The table is spread with fried chicken.
Black walnut ice cream waits in the kitchen.
Piled with the after-sleep to come.
One chair left open for these fathers,
These center-cut men who one day

Will fall like shovels from the sky.

Custody

Twelve year old girls, a basketball and a ref.
It's a curious kind of sport.
Freeze the action: stalagmites, pillars of awkward
beauty unaccustomed to motion. The player
I'm here to see is connected to me loosely.
I'm one of ten: mothers and grandmothers, half-sisters and other
half-prefixes of divorce. This ten, a courtful ourselves,
a silent and complicated offense. You can tell
which girls are better—they are tall and have mass.
The big ones, their bullying is rewarded—who can blame them?
One girl runs wishing she were alone, open
as a breezy island. The others sense her distance
and let her run. There are rules of their own making too.
The ball goes in the basket a surprising number of times.
The girl I am here to watch has her share.
She can dribble, but if challenged will immediately pass.
On offense she never demands the ball. But on defense,
no matter how large the other girl, ours gets
her hands on the ball. We begin to cheer for just this.
There is no real jump in this game—possessions
alternate. Five, six jumps. *Hooray, our girl!*
The other girls notice. They show their teeth, first in smiles,
then in snarls. Our girl's face lets nothing through.
As soon as the whistle blows, she walks away.
Eight, nine, a dozen jump balls. Our girl's a master!
She gets her hand on every ball. Fifteen, twenty!
It's beautiful and necessary. This is what she was born for.
This girl, and her unmoving face, who has a bedroom in three
houses, who shares toys and fathers and sisters,
she knows something about basketball.
She's been taught all her short life to go for the tie-up.

Bubble Screen

I stand at the window looking down,
my son tossing a football to himself.

My daughter is in the bath, splashing.
I am attending her. I attend them both.

My son says someone is here, a car.
I am on the second floor, he a story below.

I cannot see the car but I see the football.
Through the screen I tell my son to come up.

My daughter is old enough not to drown in the tub.
Probably nothing will happen.

Throughout the house are hidden gifts given,
bulbous, tenuous, breakable, paint-globbed.

It's hard to remember when these gifts were made
and what it is I am supposed to give back.

My son makes it up the stairs and gives me the ball.
I lift out the screen. Go back outside I tell him.

I don't think this is a very good idea he says,
and I say sometimes you have to do things like this.

There are three plastic men in the tub bobbing,
at the mercy of the girl's waves and their legless bodies.

A forty-year-old red maple defends the yard
and the opening is large enough for only a flick.

The ball sails at a tilt, but spiraling tight,
down to the waiting arms of my son.

It's time to drain the tub and negotiate
the climb out, terrycloth the landing.

I stand in the breech. I could leap out the window.
I could dive, pump the water from her lungs.

The catch is made not as pretty as any of us hoped
but he turns and hustles toward the yard's end zone.

Of course I checked to see if there was really a car.
Of course I celebrated. I do, every fake touchdown.

I Have Trusted

I have trusted the smell of bread. I have trusted in the promise of hours. I have trusted in emptiness. I have trusted in repair. I have trusted the wind to remove the dead. I have trusted in the other side. I trust voice and echo. I have trusted animals and have been kept whole. I have trusted the invisible. I have trusted in cars and I have walked the sides of roads. I have trusted the bees and now I give them my children. I have trusted blankness and the order of words. I trust humiliation and beards. I have never trusted water. I have trusted the arc of a basketball, the camaraderie of sweat. I have trusted plumbers. I have trusted hands. I have trusted miracle. I trust the old songs. I have trusted in doing without. I have never met hope. I have rushed to the side of fear and have trusted in nearness. I have trusted in guardians and in the thin lie of my own guardianship. I have trusted in brands and ritual. I have trusted oil and the desperate prayer. I trust age. Leave graves for the young to trust. I have trusted that forgiveness wears out and anger gets bored. I trust in periphery. I trust there is a core. I trust widely. I have not trusted enough.

The Woman Attends Her Own Death

The woman when she is young sits by the bed
Of the woman when she is old. She knows
What she should do. She puts balm on her lips,
Dabs her tongue with water, whispers a song.

The woman by the bedside has thought of
How her death would go. She sees the drawn
Sockets, the purpling nail beds, reaching jaw.
This woman doesn't know her own mind.

She coughs matchsticks. The tissue reddens.
She holds her own hand. The dying arm pulls.
A machine puffs in the hallway. Elbows,
Hard as flint. So much heat because we all

Die differently. The young die differently.
Dies with her eyes. Then her eyes die, too.

The Litany of the Body

In the end when we are asked what we have done
with all that we've been given first comes
the litany of the body. Each joint

has a name and each bone but don't worry
the names of each will be provided.
First you will start from the fragile knuckle

of the index finger to the soft tip
and like a movie the choices will come back
which means all the things you've done with this part

of your gift and the things undone and never
considered alike. This account will not
be full of regrets you will have moments

of terrible pride. Many will be known
by their elbows, the balance of injuries
received and those inflicted. The jawbone

will take the longest and even those who can't
sing will have to sing the ugliest parts.
The heel, and what we have lifted ourselves

up on. The hips and all the dances would bring
tears to your eyes if you had eyes still. Last
we come to the knee. The wind will pick up

and you will recall all the times that knee
has bent and the times it has refused to bend
and the times it bent sincerely and the times

it bent for vanity or fear. You will
remember the places it did and did not
bend and because this is the last accounting

it is the one that will keep ringing along
to the same song that you knew from the start,
that the knee, it only bends one way.

An Ordinary Season

Time to putty the windows, scrape the old,
Slather on new paint and hammer the storms.

The leaves on the tree outside your window,
The ones that stay, hang like they've been harnessed.

The snow will pile to the sill. You will run
Your fingers checking for dents in the wood.

The tree will scratch its branch, play you a tune.
Stay inside, it says, nothing needs you here.

When you leave, the tree does not speak of you.
It never knew how close it was to the heat.

Signs go up through town, roads out, bridges down.
You rest, blanket rolled, and plot out the cold.

The yellow hydrant, three-snouted, paint chipped,
Squats above, waits for the fires to come.

The children will play hockey in the street.
Nothing red like the red in their cheeks.

Fumes from the neighbor's blower char the ground.
The big plow's ruts in the road kill the game.

Press of trucks regiment the deep snowpack.
Come spring, you'll chip at the ice to find drains.

What's left of the season will begin trickling.
The ice you grasp, but not its time to melting.

How long for the sun to make its return.
Each year longer, a mind's length farther away.

The young neighbors string bulbs on the low pickets,
Petals of color arranged like a choir.

You wonder, will the boards hold, the glass stand,
If winter's house is a spell meant to break.

Whatever earth might have carried these rocks.
What difficult clouds these that stretch the sky.

When night falls the tired streets glaze blacker,
This spread of night come layered and low.

When the time comes, will the cold things inside
Of you light up, as they should, for no reason?

Where the Eulogies Gather

I wish I could tell you we were going somewhere special tonight,
that's why I chipped the ice off the car, so you and I could ride
to that place we used to talk about. I wish I could tell you that place
was still there, with the waitress and the neon tube lights and the cheese
dripping into the fries. I wish I could tell you there weren't children
upstairs, bored, waiting to razz us with our staggering dullness.
I wish I could tell you that the river was still there, running along
the highway in a race to hide itself. To be the first to die.
I wish I could tell you there was a prize in being the first,
that the survivors get together in rectangles to honor your exit.
I wish I could tell you no one will go through our house,
or disturb those knick knacks or crackle the hidden papers.
They will all be touched. I wish I could tell you nothing matters.
That we're all covered with a kind of ice, thickening with time,
sometimes brittle, others unbreakable. I wish I could tell you
your friends will always love you. That they will always be
in the place you left them. That they will want to break through.
I wish I could tell you that all we have is paint, that we leave
our tracks wherever we go. The world is full of blank museums.
I wish I could tell you we were still wild, that your best self
won't need to be quarantined. That you'll keep your teeth.
I wish I could tell you that when your body breaks
each bone will have a bearer, that each will know
where to take it, that they will arrive at the same place.
I wish I could tell you that we're in this together,
that I know the shape of the vessel, that it looks like us,
that when you reach out, you will feel something holding you.
I wish I could tell you that no one knows the exact words you do,
not even the hairs that have left your head. If I told the truth instead,
I would tell you I was just moving the car for the plow.
I would tell you the car left a car-sized spot on the pavement,
where no snow or ice gathered. This is where the eulogies go,
felled like snow then salted away underneath our cars.
They begin as soon as they pass the lips. They arrive
without our knowing, before words, in the shape of absence.
This is the raft we will ride. It is the raft we have always ridden.

Acknowledgments

Thanks to my family. My mom, who made poetry of the overlooked. My dad, who shook walnuts from his pocket. My brother Scott, who also knows what it means to be from my Oklahoma. My wife Alecia, first reader, best reader. My children Isaac and Charlotte, who help me see the world differently.

Thanks to the editors of publications these poems appeared in, particularly *Cincinnati Review, Juked* and *Ruminate* for nominating them for awards.

Thanks to Dean Rader, who provided valuable feedback from the beginning. Thanks to everyone in Poet's Choice and the April poetry group: Aaron Brossiet, Katie Cappello, Ashley Cardona, Brian Clements, Brian Komei Dempster, Judy Halebsky, Mike Henry, Amorak Huey, Todd Kaneko, Amy McInnis, Ander Monson, Christina Olson, Jean Prokott, Mark Schaub, Gale Thompson.

Thanks to my teachers and friends, especially those who taught me the most about poetry: Edward Hirsch, Averill Curdy, Ryan Iwanaga, Pablo Peschiera, Patty Seyburn.

Thanks to Raymond Hammond, for rescuing these poems.

Thanks to my Grand Valley State University colleagues and to my hard-working and inspiring students.

And thanks to all of you for reading.

Previous Publications

The following poems appeared in these publications, sometimes in a slightly different form.

Apalachee Review:	The War Photographer, 2015
Barely South Review:	Pocket Walnuts, 2017
Beloit Poetry Journal:	Instant Replay, 2015-16
Blackbird:	The Boy Shows the Girl His Country, 2012; Carry On and We are at a feast which doesn't love us, 2018
BOXCAR Poetry Review:	The President Declares Disaster, 2016
Cider Press Review:	I Have Trusted, 2019
Cimarron Review	We Could Use Some Milk, 2020
Cincinnati Review:	The Woman Attends Her Own Death, 2017
Clockhouse:	Lovers Resolve, Charles and Emma Darwin, 2015
Colorado Review:	Bounty, 2015
ellipsis:	Winter Tomato: To Depression, 2015
Fence:	Purple Berries, 2018
Front Porch Journal:	Flannery at Lourdes, 2014
Gargoyle:	How Nuclear Fusion Works, 2011; The Cake Girl, 2013
The Golden Shovel Anthology: New Poems Honoring Gwendolyn Brooks:	The dark hangs heavily, 2017
Grasslimb:	The Difficulty of Simultaneity, 2013
The Grove Review:	Say This in the Coming Storm, 2012
Hawai'I Review:	I Am the Watchman, 2016
The Hollins Critic:	Tombstone, 2014
Interim:	Discussion Questions on the Dead Man, Sophomore Literature and Poem for the Recent Tragedy, 2018
Juked:	Elegies on the Passing of Celebrity, 2011
KNOCK:	Sandman, 2011
Linebreak:	Janis Joplin's Eulogy to the Graduating Class of Thomas Jefferson High in Port Arthur, Texas, 1960, 2011

Louisville Review: Bubble Screen, 2013

Minnesota Review: Jonestown, 2013

Nimrod: The Word We're Looking for is Sorry, 2013

NOÖ Journal: The Best Among Us, 2011

The Normal School: A Thousand Sexy Wives, 2010

Parcel: The Fence, 2016

Pebble Lake Review: Who among you is afraid to go into the dark and empty spaces? 2009

Pleiades: Interrogative; Ocean, 2016

Poet Lore: Custody, 2011

Poet's Market 2014:   Five Ways of Looking at a Mushroom Cloud, 2013

Ruminate: Litany of the Body, 2020

Sentence: Phony London, 2010

Smartish Pace: The Iceberg and the Volcano; Middle Space, 2011

Spillway: Bead Board, 2018

The Southern Review: The Second Pig, 2018.

Stoneboat: Uses for the Appendix, 2014

storySouth: The Outlaw Pose, 2017

Thin Air: The Black Hole Uploads a Match.com Profile, 2014

Zócalo Public Square: The Songbird's Song, 2010; reprinted *The Michigan Poet*, 2011; reprinted *The Michigan Poet: Collected Poems*, 2016

www.ingramcontent.com/pod-product-compliance
Lightning Source LLC
Chambersburg PA
CBHW022014080426
42733CB00007B/593